SCHOLASTIC

writing guides

With interactive resources on CD-ROM

Fairy Stories

for ages
5-7

Louise Carruthers,
Hilary Braund and
Deborah Gibbon

Terms and conditions

Credits

Authors
Louise Carruthers, Hilary Braund and Deborah Gibbon

Series Consultant
Huw Thomas

Development Editor
Simret Brar

Editor
Gaynor Spry

Assistant Editors
Vicky Butt, Marion Archer and Pam Kelt

Series Designer
Anna Oliwa, Micky Pledge

Designers
Helen Taylor and Paul Stockmans

Cover Illustration
Mark Oliver

Illustrations
Tim Archbold

CD-ROM Development
CD-ROM developed in association with Infuze Ltd

Text © Louise Carruthers, Hilary Braund, Deborah Gibbon
© 2009 Scholastic Ltd

Designed using Adobe InDesign

Published by Scholastic Ltd,
Villiers House,
Clarendon Avenue,
LeamingtonSpa,
Warwickshire
CV32 5PR

www.scholastic.co.uk

Printed by Bell & Bain

1 2 3 4 5 6 7 8 9   9 0 1 2 3 4 5 6 7 8 9

British Library Cataloguing-in-Publication Data
A catalogue record for this book is available from the British Library.

ISBN 978-1407-11253-4

The rights of Louise Carruthers, Hilary Braund and Deborah Gibbon to be identified as the authors of this work have been asserted by them in accordance with the Copyright, Designs and Patents Act 1988.

Extracts from the Primary National Strategy's Primary Framework for Literacy (2006) www.standards.dfes.gov.uk/primaryframework © Crown copyright. Reproduced under the terms of the Click Use Licence.

Acknowledgements
Andersen Press for the use of an extract from *Little Red Riding Hood* by Tony Ross © 1978, Tony Ross (1978, Andersen). **HarperCollins Publishers** for the use of extracts 'Little Red Riding Hood' and 'Goldilocks and the Three Bears' from *Classic Fairy Tales* by Helen Creswell © 1993, Helen Creswell (1993, HarperCollins) and an extract from *Little Red Riding Hood* by Jonathan Langley © 1992, Jonathan Langley (1992, HarperCollins).

Every effort has been made to trace copyright holders of the works reproduced in this book, and the publishers apologise for any inadvertent omissions.

Mixed Sources
Product group from well-managed forests and other controlled sources
www.fsc.org Cert no. TT-COC-002769
© 1996 Forest Stewardship Council
FSC

CD-ROM Minimum specifications:

Windows 2000/XP/Vista		Mac OSX 10.4
Processor: 1 GHz	RAM: 512 MB	Graphics card: 32bit
Audio card: Yes	CD-ROM drive speed: 8x	Hard disk space: 200MB
Screen resolution: 800x600		

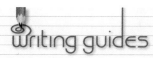

Contents

Introduction: Fairy Stories

The *Writing Guides* series aims to inspire and motivate children as writers by using creative approaches. Each *Writing Guide* contains activities and photocopiable resources designed to develop children's understanding of a particular genre (for example, fairy stories). The activities are in line with the requirements of the National Curriculum and the recommendations in the *Primary Framework for Literacy*. The teacher resource books are accompanied by a CD-ROM containing a range of interactive activities and resources.

What's in the book?

The *Writing Guides* series provides a structured approach to developing children's writing. Each book is divided into four sections.

Section 1: **Using good examples**
Three text extracts are provided to explore the typical features of the genre.

Section 2: **Developing writing**
There are ten short, focussed writing tasks in this section. These are designed to develop children's ability to use the key features of the genre in their own writing. The teacher's notes explain the objective of each activity and provide guidance on delivery, including how to use the photocopiable pages and the materials on the CD-ROM.

Section 3: **Writing**
The three writing projects in this section require the children to produce an extended piece of writing using the key features of the genre.

Section 4: **Review**
This section consists of a 'Self review', 'Peer review' and 'Teacher review'. These can be used to evaluate how effectively the children have met the writing criteria for the genre.

What's on the CD-ROM?

The accompanying CD-ROM contains a range of motivating activities and resources. The activities can be used for independent work or can be used on an interactive whiteboard to enhance group teaching.
Each CD-ROM contains:

- three text extracts that illustrate the typical features of the genre
- interactive versions of selected photocopiable pages
- four photographs and an audio file to create imaginative contexts for writing
- a selection of writing templates and images which can be used to produce extended pieces of writing.

The interactive activities on the CD-ROM promote active learning and support a range of teaching approaches and learning styles. For example, drag and drop and sequencing activities will support kinaesthic learners.

Talk for writing

Each *Writing Guide* uses the principles of 'Talk for writing' to support children's writing development by providing opportunities for them to rehearse ideas orally in preparation for writing. 'Talk for writing' is promoted using a variety of teaching strategies including discussions, questioning and drama activities (such as, developing imaginative dialogue – see *Fantasy Stories for Ages 9–11*).

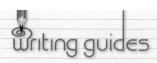

How to use the CD-ROM

Start screen: click on the 'Start' button to go to the main menu.

This section contains brief instructions on how to use the CD-ROM. For more detailed guidance, go to 'How to use the CD-ROM' on the start screen or click on the 'Help' button located in the top right-hand corner of the screen.

Installing the CD-ROM

Follow the instructions on the disk to install the CD-ROM onto your computer. Once the CD-ROM is installed, navigate to the program location and double click on the program icon to open it.

Main menu screen

Main menu

The main menu provides links to all of the writing activities and resources on the CD-ROM. Clicking on a button from the main menu will take you to a sub-menu that lists all of the activities and resources in that section. From here you have the option to 'Launch' the interactive activities, which may contain more than one screen, or print out the activities for pupils to complete by hand.

If you wish to return to a previous menu, click the 'Menu' button in the top right-hand corner of the screen; this acts as a 'back' button.

Screen tools

A range of simple writing tools that can be used in all of the writing activities are contained in the toolbar at the bottom of the screen.

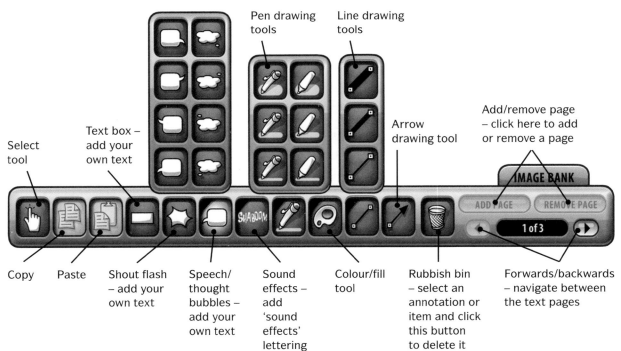

Pen drawing tools

Line drawing tools

Add/remove page – click here to add or remove a page

Select tool

Text box – add your own text

Arrow drawing tool

Copy

Paste

Shout flash – add your own text

Speech/ thought bubbles – add your own text

Sound effects – add 'sound effects' lettering

Colour/fill tool

Rubbish bin – select an annotation or item and click this button to delete it

Forwards/backwards – navigate between the text pages

How to use the CD-ROM

Print

Save your work to chosen files

Open – navigate to your saved file to open your previous work

Reset the page

Printing and saving work

All of the resources on the CD-ROM are printable. You can also save and retrieve any annotations made on the writing activities. Click on the 'Controls' tab on the right-hand side of the screen to access the 'Print', 'Open', 'Save' and 'Reset screen' buttons.

View all thumbnails by clicking on the arrows

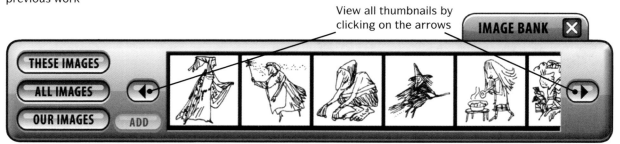

Image bank – click and drag an image to add it to an activity

Image bank

Each CD-ROM has an 'Image bank' containing images appropriate to the genre being taught. Click on the tab at the bottom right of the screen to open the 'Image bank'. On the left-hand side there are three large buttons.

- The 'These images' button will display only the images associated with the specific activity currently open.
- The 'All images' button will display all the photographs and illustrations available on the CD-ROM.
- The 'Our images' button will contain any images you or the children have added to the CD-ROM.

Press the left or right arrows to scroll through the images available. Select an image and drag and drop it into the desired location on the screen. If necessary, resize the image using the arrow icon that appears at the bottom right of the image.

You can upload images to the 'Image bank', including digital photographs or images drawn and scanned into the computer. Click on 'Our images' and then 'Add' to navigate to where the image is stored. A thumbnail picture will be added to the gallery.

Writing your own story

Each CD-ROM contains a selection of blank writing templates. The fiction genre templates will be categorised under the button 'My story' and the non-fiction templates will be categorised under 'My recount' or 'My writing'. The writing templates encourage the children to produce an extended piece of genre writing. They can also add images, speech bubbles and use other tools to enhance their work.

The fiction titles also include a cover template for the children to use. They can customise their cover by adding their own title, blurb and images.

Section 1
Using good examples

Using fairy stories

Fairy stories provide a wealth of opportunities for developing children's story writing. The content is familiar to children and the stylised language makes the story comfortable, predictable and enjoyable, even when told and retold.

Fairy tales tend to have a distinctive narrative plot. Recurring themes can be identified, such as the struggles between rich and poor, good and evil, and wise and foolish. The number three is an important number in many fairy tales. Stories often have three characters or a single event may be repeated three times. Fairytale endings where everything turns out for the best are common.

Fairytale characters typically represent the archetypical opposites of good and evil, wise and foolish, or hero and villain. They may include humans, animals or other creatures often with magical powers.

Castles, cottages and woods are common settings. Information about when events took place is often vague (once upon a time, long ago). The style of traditional fairy stories is strongly influenced by their origins in oral storytelling. The box on the left summarises their key structural and language features.

Through shared reading of a range of complete fairy stories and the extracts on photocopiable pages 10–13 and on the CD-ROM, children will gain valuable experience of the key conventions of the fairytale genre (which they can draw on in their own texts).

As well as perennial favourites, try to include less well-known stories, for example 'The Golden Goose', 'Snow White and Rose Red' and 'Mrs Goat and Her Seven Little Kids'.

Fairy tales and the Primary Framework

The Literacy Framework states that developing understanding of and having opportunities to write narrative texts is a fundamental aspect of children's literacy development. The framework provides detailed guidance for teaching and learning about fairy tales at Key Stage 1 (Year 1: Narrative Units 2 and 3, Year 2: Narrative Unit 3).

The activities in this book address objectives from all 12 strands of the Literacy Framework but with a particular focus on strands 7–10 (Understanding and interpreting texts, Engaging with and responding to texts, Creating and shaping texts, Text structure and organisation).

Fairytale features

Structure
Fairy tales tend to have a distinctive narrative plot:
- beginning – a setting and characters are introduced
- middle – a dilemma or conflict is introduced, and a chronological series of events occur that resolve the situation
- end – the narrative is drawn to a close.

Style
Most fairy stories use:
- the third person and the past tense
- temporal connectives ('once', 'finally')
- rich descriptive vocabulary
- repetitive language patterns and repeated refrains
- formulaic openings and endings.

Extract 1: 'Little Red Riding Hood'

What's on the CD-ROM

Little Red Riding Hood
- Text extracts to read and discuss.

What's the same?
- Drag and drop the statements that apply to all three story openings into the box.

These three introductions to 'Little Red Riding Hood' illustrate common features of fairytale openings and different versions of the same story.

- Read or tell a version of 'Little Red Riding Hood'.

- Open the CD-ROM file 'Little Red Riding Hood' and read the three story introductions. Talk about why the beginning of a story is important. Ask: *Which introduction makes you want to read on and why?*

- Organise the children into small groups. Give each group a copy of photocopiable page 14 'Starting the story' and ask them to explore the introductory paragraphs in greater detail. Take feedback and record the key points on the board. Children can then complete the photocopiable in small groups.

- Analyse the information in the completed tables to identify similarities and differences between the three extracts. Identify what additional details each author has included to make his or her story opening unique.

- Open the CD-ROM file 'What's the same?' Set the children on individual computers to identify the statements that apply to all three story introductions (drag and drop) or ask them to complete the same activity using photocopiable page 15 'What's the same?'

- Ask the children to plan and write their own opening to 'Little Red Riding Hood', with details of their own to make their version unique.

Extract 2: 'Goldilocks'

What's on the CD-ROM

Goldilocks and the Three Bears
- Text extract to read and discuss.

What did they say?
- Fill in the speech bubbles to show what the three bears are saying.

The second extract looks at the patterned language, particularly in speech, that is a characteristic feature of many traditional fairy tales.

- Read or tell a version of 'Goldilocks and the Three Bears'.

- Open the CD-ROM file 'Goldilocks and the Three Bears' and display the extract from Helen Cresswell's retelling on the whiteboard. Read it to the class using appropriate expression and intonation for each of the characters' voices. Discuss how the repetition encourages the reader/listener to participate in the telling of the story.

- Open the CD-ROM file 'What did they say?' For each of the two screens, ask the children to suggest what they think each bear is saying. Act as scribe or invite different children to type their ideas into the speech bubbles. Emphasise that you are using the patterned language from the extract to structure the writing. Draw attention to spelling strategies and sentence structure including capital letters and different forms of punctuation, and encourage the children to help with spelling.

- Hand out copies of photocopiable page 16 'What did they say?' to the children. Ask them to work in pairs and suggest what the bears said.

- Explore other fairy stories with repeated phrases, for example 'The Gingerbread Man', 'Rapunzel' and 'Jack and the Beanstalk'.

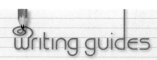

Extract 3: 'Sleeping Beauty'

What's on the CD-ROM

Sleeping Beauty
● Text extract to read and discuss.

Time connectives
● Add the missing time connectives.

Analysis of the third extract will allow children to investigate how the language of time can be used to sequence and structure narrative writing.

● Read or tell a version of 'Sleeping Beauty'. Track the main plot sequence and predict what will happen next at different points in the story. Ask: *Will the princess die? Who might save the princess? How?*

● Open the CD-ROM file 'Sleeping Beauty' and display the extract. Ask the children to highlight all the time connectives in the text. Discuss how some of these words are used to indicate time ('after', 'many years later') and others ('suddenly') to create impact for the reader.

● Encourage the children to think of alternative time connectives to the ones used in the story and to type them in. For example, change 'Long, long ago' to 'Many years ago', or change 'at once' to 'immediately'. Read the edited version of the text together. Consider whether each of the words and phrases are suitable. Ask the children whether they think they have improved the text. If so, why?

● Display the activity 'Time connectives' from the CD-ROM on the whiteboard. Work together with the class using the time connectives at the bottom of the screen to complete the sentences. Alternatively, give out copies of photocopiable page 17 'Time connectives' for the children to complete independently.

● In shared writing, model how to continue the story using a range of connectives to link ideas and build tension. Make a class bank of time connectives collected from stories read.

Poster: Fairy tales

What's on the CD-ROM

Fairy tales poster
● Read and discuss the information on the poster.
● Hover over each section to display further rollover text.

● Display the interactive 'Fairy tales poster' on the CD-ROM. Explore the information presented in each section of the poster to promote discussion of some of the key narrative features of the genre. Hover over each area to display the further rollover text.

● Discuss each element in turn, making references to 'Little Red Riding Hood', 'Goldilocks and the Three Bears' and 'Sleeping Beauty' before extending the class discussion to include other known fairy tales, many of which are referred to on the poster. Then, discuss the content of each story with reference to the interactive poster to develop the children's understanding of and familiarity with all the main elements of the genre.

● You can also make use of the poster as a planning and evaluation tool to support children's independent writing. Give each child their own copy of photocopiable page 18 'Fairy tales poster' to use as a reminder and prompt sheet to ensure they include all the key features of the genre when planning and writing their own fairy stories.

Extract 1: 'Little Red Riding Hood'

Three story introductions

Once upon a time, on the edge of the big wood, there lived a little girl called Little Red Riding Hood. Her real name was Brenda but she was always known as Little Red Riding Hood because this was what her mother called her when she was a baby. Brenda used to wear a red bonnet when she went for a ride in her pram, and she still wears it now.

One day Little Red Riding Hood was playing out in the sunshine when her mother called her: "I want you to go over to Grandma's house with some groceries. Grandma's not very well and she hasn't been able to get out to the shops."

Jonathan Langley

Text © 1992, Jonathan Langley. Illustrations © 2009, Tim Archibold.

Extract 1: 'Little Red Riding Hood'

Three story introductions continued

Once upon a time, a little girl lived on the edge of the forest. Her dad was a woodcutter, whose job it was to hack down trees so that all sorts of things, like houses and comics, could be made from the wood.

Sometimes the little girl would help her dad in his work; she even had her own little axe. The woodcutter enjoyed his daughter's help. They were very close.

Once a week, the little girl visited her grandma, who lived deep in the deepest forest.

Tony Ross

Once upon a time there was a little girl whose father was a woodcutter in a big forest. Her mother had made her a cloak and hood of bright red wool, and she wore it so often that she was known as Little Red Riding Hood.

One day her mother called her and said, "Your grandmother is not well today. I have made some little cakes and put them in this basket, and there's a pat of butter and some new laid eggs. I want you to take them to her and see how she is. But mind you go straight there and back and don't go off the path."

Helen Cresswell

Extract 2: 'Goldilocks and the Three Bears'

Then the bears went upstairs.
"Someone has been lying in my bed," growled the Great Rough Bear in his great rough voice.

"Someone has been lying in my bed, too," said the Mother Bear in her soft mother voice.

"Someone has been lying in my bed and here she is!" cried the Wee Small Bear in his shrill small voice.

Just then Goldilocks awoke. She saw the big furry faces of the three bears looking down at her, and with a loud shriek jumped up and rushed down the stairs and out of the cottage with her hair flying out behind her.

"She is afraid of us!" laughed the Great Rough Bear in his great rough voice.

"She is afraid of us!" laughed the Mother Bear in her soft mother voice.

"She is afraid of us!" laughed the Wee Small Bear in his wee shrill way.

As for Goldilocks, she didn't stop to draw breath till she was safely home again. And she never again went into a house when she found the door standing open, because for all she knew those three bears might have gobbled her up. How was she to know they only liked porridge and wild honey?

Helen Cresswell

Text © 1993, Helen Cresswell. Illustrations © 2009, Tim Archibold.

Extract 3: 'Sleeping Beauty'

Long, long ago in a faraway land, lived a wealthy king and queen. The king and queen lived in a splendid palace with many precious treasures. In spite of their great riches the king and queen were unhappy as, more than anything else, they longed for a child.

At last, many years later, the queen gave birth to a beautiful baby girl. The king was at once the happiest man in the world. He ordered a lavish feast to celebrate her christening. After the feast, 12 good fairies who were to be the child's godmothers each bestowed a special gift on the little princess so that when she grew up she would be blessed with beauty, intelligence, courage and many other special qualities.

Suddenly, as the twelfth fairy approached the child's cradle, the palace doors burst open and an uninvited fairy swept into the great hall. Unlike the other fairies she was old and wizened and when she spoke it was in a harsh, croaky voice:

"You did not invite me to be a fairy godmother to your child so I will cast a spell on her. When she is 15 she will prick her finger with a spindle and drop down dead instantly." Then, as quickly as the wicked fairy had appeared, she vanished without trace from the palace.

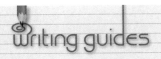

Section 1: Using good examples

Starting the story

● Read the three 'Little Red Riding Hood' extracts. Use this table to record the information given by each of the authors in their story introduction.

	What is the setting?	What characters are included?	What information is given about Little Red Riding Hood?
Jonathon Langley			
Tony Ross			
Helen Cresswell			

writing guides

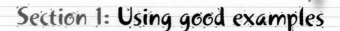
What's the same?

● Cut out and stick into the box the statements that are true about all three versions of 'Little Red Riding Hood'.

Little Red Riding Hood had a little brother.
Little Red Riding Hood wore a red hat or hood.
Little Red Riding Hood's father was a woodcutter.
Little Red Riding Hood lived in a castle.
Little Red Riding Hood went to visit her grandfather .
Little Red Riding Hood had a little axe.
Little Red Riding Hood lived next door to her grandma.
Little Red Riding Hood lived 'once upon a time'.

What did they say?

- Complete these speech bubbles for the three bears.
Write in your own words, but use the pattern of language in the extract as a guide.

Illustrations © 2009, Tim Archibold.

Time connectives

● Cut out the labels below and match them to the sentences.

_____ a king and queen lived in a faraway place.

_____ a bad fairy appeared.

_____ the princess was 15 she pricked her finger on a spindle.

_____ a handsome prince woke sleeping beauty.

| One hundred years later |

| Once upon a time |

| Suddenly |

| When |

Illustrations © 2009, Tim Archibold.

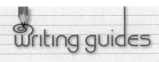

Fairy tales

Setting	Characters	Plot
When does the story take place?	**Which characters are good or bad?**	**Beginning**
Where does the story take place?	**What do they say?**	**Middle** **Happy endings**

Illustrations © 2009, Tim Archibold.

Section 2
Developing writing

Activities breakdown

The activities in this section provide opportunities for children to explore the key elements of the fairytale genre in terms of character, setting and plot. The distinctive language of fairy stories is also examined through the analysis of dialogue, time connectives and story language and by playing with repeated phrases and synonyms.

Character

Children are given opportunities to discuss and write about the appearance, actions and behaviour of characters in a wide range of fairy stories. Drama techniques such as role play and hot-seating are used to help children to develop empathy with characters and speculate on how they might feel and behave in different situtations.

Setting

Four typical fairy story settings are introduced using the photographs and the audio clip on the CD-ROM as stimulus. The children are asked to think of words to describe the appearance and atmosphere of each story setting which they are then encouraged to use in their own writing.

Plot

The pattern of story development, from the introduction through to the climax and resolution, is mapped out using well-known fairy tales. The children will have opportunities to retell stories and to sequence the main events in fairy tales they know well.

How to use the activities

Detailed teachers' notes giving guidance on delivery, including how to use the photocopiable pages at the end of the section and the materials on the CD-ROM, support each activity. Children are encouraged to write in a range of forms and a variety of simple writing templates are provided to scaffold the development of their independent writing. Through discussion activities, retelling and role play, the children get opportunities to rehearse their ideas orally before writing them down. The activities are highly flexible and can be adapted. All the activities should be modelled for the whole class or smaller groups using the whiteboard before the children are asked to undertake any independent work.

Activities breakdown

Character
- Fairytale characters
- Catchphrase
- Wicked ideas
- Cinderella's feelings

Setting
- Describe the setting
- Who lives here?

Plot
- Order the story
- The plot
- Here we go again!
- Beginnings and endings

Activity 1: Fairytale characters

Objective

To make adventurous word and language choices appropriate to the style and purpose of the text (Year 2 Strand 9).

What's on the CD-ROM

Fairytale characters
- Drag and drop adjectives into a table.
- Make a collection of words and phrases that describe a familiar fairytale character.

What to do

This activity encourages children to describe and discuss the features and characteristics of some well-known fairytale characters.

- Read 'Little Red Riding Hood' to the children. Highlight words and phrases in the text that describe the wolf's appearance and character. Encourage the children to express their own opinions about the wolf, drawing on their knowledge of the story to support their views, for example: *I think the wolf is cunning because he puts on a disguise to trick Red Riding Hood.* List some of the children's ideas on the board.

- Open the CD-ROM file 'Fairytale characters'. Read screen 1 and clarify any unfamiliar words. Invite different children to drag and drop one of the adjectives from the box into the correct part of the table.

- Look at screen 2 on the CD-ROM. Insert a fairytale character from the 'Image bank' into the picture frame. Ask children to think of words to describe the character. Type some of their suggestions into the scrolls.

- Ask individual or pairs of children to complete photocopiable page 25 'Fairytale characters' for a fairytale character of their choice.

Activity 2: Catchphrase / Say that again

Objective

To compose and write simple sentences independently to communicate meaning (Year 1 Strand 11).

What's on the CD-ROM

Catchphrase
- Drag arrows from fairytale characters to the correct speech bubble.

What to do

This lesson looks at the use of repeated dialogue in fairy stories.

- Open the CD-ROM file 'Catchphrase'. Read the dialogue in each speech bubble with expression and intonation. Together, identify which fairy tale each phrase comes from and which character says the words. Invite four different children to drag an arrow from one character to the correct speech bubble. Alternatively, hand out copies of photocopiable page 26 'Catchphrase' and ask the children to match the speech bubble to the correct fairytale character.

- Explore the dialogue in more detail. Consider how each catchphrase is repeated by the character at several different points during the story, making it memorable for the storyteller/reader. Encourage the children to notice the use of rhyme and alliteration to add interest.

- Hand out copies of photocopiable page 27 'Say that again'. Ask the children to recall the repeated phrase spoken by Little Red Riding Hood and the Little Pig and write suggestions into each speech bubble.

- Invite the children to invent their own character and catchphrase. Encourage more confident children to experiment with adjectives, rhymes or alliteration to add interest to dialogue. Less confident children could draw and write the catchphrase for another well-known fairytale character, such as the Gingerbread Man.

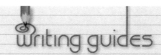

Activity 3: Wicked ideas

Objective

To explore familiar themes and characters through improvisation and role play (Year 1 Strand 4).

What to do

Children will explore the motives and behaviour of nasty fairytale characters.

- Ask the children to make a list of wicked characters from fairy tales.

- Hand out copies of photocopiable page 28 'Wicked ideas'. Focus on the wolf first, identify him and which fairy tale he comes from. Recall the bad things he does and says and ask the children to consider why he might act in this way. Use drama techniques to explore the wolf's motives and behaviour in greater depth.

- Ask the children to imagine what the wolf is thinking. Working in pairs, let the children draft their ideas on their sheets before feeding back to the others. Write one of the children's suggestions in a thought bubble on the board. Model how to add emphasis by using bold print, capitalisation or exclamation marks.

- Then move on to focus on the giant and witch.

- Ask the children to write a sentence in each of the thought bubbles on photocopiable page 28 to show what the characters are plotting.

- Finally, let the children invent their own character with a wicked idea!

Activity 4: Cinderella's feelings

Objective

To present part of traditional stories, their own stories or work drawn from different parts of the curriculum for members of their own class (Year 2 Strand 4).

What to do

The children are encouraged to make predictions about how a character's feelings and behaviour can change during the course of a story.

- Read or tell the story of 'Cinderella' to the children. Pause at significant points in the story to discuss what is happening and predict what will happen next. Encourage the children to empathise with the character of Cinderella and to consider how her feelings change in response to things that are said to her and events she experiences.

- Hand out copies of photocopiable page 29 'Cinderella's feelings' and discuss the first image. Ask the children in groups of four to act out this part of the story with appropriate dialogue, including expression and intonation. Allow one or more groups to present their role play to the class. Ask children to volunteer ideas about what each character is thinking/saying. Write some of the children's suggestions in thought and speech bubbles on the board.

- Repeat the above for the second image.

- Ask the children to complete photocopiable page 29 'Cinderella's feelings' with their own ideas.

- For an extension activity, ask the children to draw a picture of the happy ending and add speech and thought bubbles.

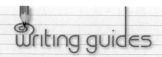

Activity 5: Describe the setting

Objective

To choose words for effect, making writing interesting for the reader
(Year 2 writing targets).

What's on the CD-ROM

Media resources
- Look at and describe four photographs.
- Listen to the audio clip.

Describe the setting
- Complete sentences to describe a setting.

What to do

In this activity children are encouraged to imagine and describe the features and atmosphere of a typical fairytale setting.

- Using the four photographs in the 'Media resources' section of the CD-ROM, ask the children to briefly describe each of the settings.

- Take the class on an imaginary journey into the woodland setting. Play the audio clip 'A woodland sound'. Ask: *Look around. What can you see? Listen carefully. What can you hear? What can you smell? How do you feel?* Encourage really inventive and imaginative language choices.

- Open the CD-ROM file 'Describe the setting'. Select a setting from 'These images' in the 'Image bank'. Encourage the children to select appropriate words and phrases to complete each of the sentences on both screens. Type in some of the children's ideas. Draw attention to sentence construction, in particular basic sentence grammar and punctuation.

- Provide each child with a copy of photocopiable page 30 'Describe the setting'. Ask them to draw a picture of the setting which has been discussed and to complete the sentences below the picture.

Activity 6: Who lives here?

Objective

To give some reasons why things happen or characters change
(Year 2 Strand 7).

What's on the CD-ROM

Who lives here?
- Image bank: Suggest what stories might happen in each setting and select one setting to explore further.
- Having selected one setting, type in answers to the onscreen questions.

What to do

The children discuss the types of characters who might live in a particular setting and how a story's setting can influence events and behaviour.

- Open the CD-ROM file 'Who lives here?' and look at the four photographs in the 'Image bank'. Ask the children to describe each place, then name different stories set in these places. Notice that the events in some stories occur in more than one location, for example 'Jack and the Beanstalk' (cottage and castle).

- Focus on one of the settings. Ask the children in pairs to discuss the following: *Who lives in this place? What are they like? What might happen here?* Each pair can feed back their ideas. Reflect on how different settings can influence events and behaviour.

- Select one of the settings from 'These images' in the 'Image bank'. Type in answers to the questions on both screens as a shared writing activity, using some of the ideas generated in the discussion activity.

- Give each child a copy of photocopiable page 31 'Who lives here?' to complete, based on one of the settings depicted in the 'Image bank', or accessed through 'Media resources'.

- Let the children describe their chosen characters and events to the class without revealing the chosen setting. Can the rest of the class guess the setting based on the information they are given?

Activity 7: Order the story

Objective

To retell stories, ordering events using story language (Year 1 Strand 1).

What's on the CD-ROM

Order the story
- Sequence the pictures in the order that they occur in the story.

What to do

The aim of this activity is to develop children's understanding of the order of events in a story and how the language of time can link events.

- Read a copy of 'Sleeping Beauty'. Encourage the children to recall what happens next at different points and to consider how the main events in the story are connected. Make deductions about why the events take place in a particular order by examining the main characters' actions and their consequences.

- Open the CD-ROM file 'Order the story'. Work together to sequence the images (in the 'These images' section of the 'Image bank')in the order that the events occur in the story. Pose simple questions on the sequential relationship between the main events: *Which picture(s) represent(s) what happened at the beginning/middle/end of the story? Could the events have occurred in a different order? Why not?*

- Give small groups a set of the plot cards on photocopiable page 32 'Order the story'. After reordering the cards, ask each group to rehearse and present a retelling of the story using the plot cards. They should include dialogue and description in their retelling and use appropriate time connectives to link the sequence of events.

- Ask the children to rewrite the story in order.

Activity 8: The plot

Objective

To recognise the main elements that shape different texts (Year 1 Strand 7).

What to do

The aim of this activity is to consolidate the children's understanding of the clearly patterned story structure found in traditional fairy tales.

- Read a version of 'Little Red Riding Hood'. Encourage the children to predict/recall what is going to happen next at different points in the story. Introduce the term 'plot' (what happens in the story). Ask the children to say which part of the plot they liked best and why. Talk about how interest and excitement is created as the plot is developed.

- Hand out copies of photocopiable page 33 'The plot' and explain that the activity requires the children to complete the plot breakdown for a different well-known fairy tale or for their own fairy story. Explain that many other fairy stories follow this plot structure: characters ➜ setting ➜ story opening ➜ problem ➜ resolution ➜ ending.

- Ask the children to suggest other fairy stories for which the plot breakdown could be filled in. Choose one that they know well and use information suggested by the children to complete the table together.

- Working either individually or in pairs, ask the children to complete a plot breakdown for a fairy story of their choice.

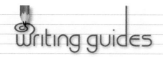

Activity 9: Here we go again!

Objective

To use key features of narrative in their own writing (Year 1 Strand 9).

What to do

This activity introduces the importance of the number three in many fairy tales, for example, three characters or three wishes being granted.

● Read a version of 'The Three Little Pigs'. Ask the children to recall the main events in the story. Write the key stages of the plot on the board using arrows to indicate sequence (characters → setting → story opening → problem → resolution → ending).

● Discuss why the number three is important in this and many other fairy stories. Ask the children to identify an event that is repeated three times in this story using the plot sequence on the board.

● Hand out copies of photocopiable page 34 'Here we go again!' and ask the children to complete the sheet to help plan their own fairy story, which includes the structure of having three characters or three main events. Stress the importance of including repetition in their story.

● Select children to read out their plans and encourage other children to provide constructive feedback.

Activity 10: Beginnings and endings

Objective

To find and use new and interesting words and phrases including story language (Year 1 Strand 9).

What to do

In this activity the children will investigate and make a collection of phrases that are typically used at the beginning and end of fairy stories.

● Read several traditional fairy stories to the class. Encourage the children to join in and recite repeated words and phrases. Make comparisons between the stories and ask the children to identify typical features.

● Create a table on the board with two columns, one with the heading 'beginnings' and the other 'endings'. Ask the children to identify examples of formal story language which have been used at the beginning and end of fairy stories. Write the phrases into the appropriate column of the table. Encourage the children to notice similarities: *Are all the stories set a long time ago in the past? Do they all have a happy ending?*

● Working in small groups, ask the children to investigate further examples for this table. Have a large collection of fairy stories available for the children to look through.

● Gather the class around the board. Record all the different beginnings and endings the children have found in the table. Encourage them to keep a lookout for further examples.

● Create a poster containing the children's findings and display it in the classroom. Encourage the children to use some of these typical story openings and endings when composing their own stories.

 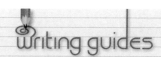

Fairytale characters

● Choose a fairytale character to draw in the picture frame. Think of some words to describe the character you have chosen. Write the words in the table below.

Appearance	Characteristics

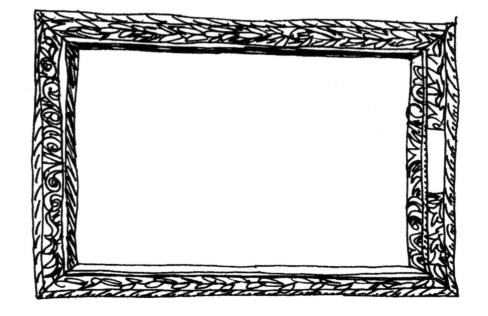

Section 2: Developing writing

Catchphrase

● Draw a line from each speech bubble to the correct fairytale character.

Who's that trip-trapping over my bridge?

Fee-Fi-Fo-Fum, I smell the blood of an Englishman.

Who's been eating my porridge?

I'll huff and I'll puff and I'll blow your house down!

Illustrations © 2009, Tim Archibold.

Say that again

● Fill in the speech bubbles to show what each of these characters is well known for saying.

● Draw a new fairytale character on the back of this page. Write a catchphrase for your character in a speech bubble.

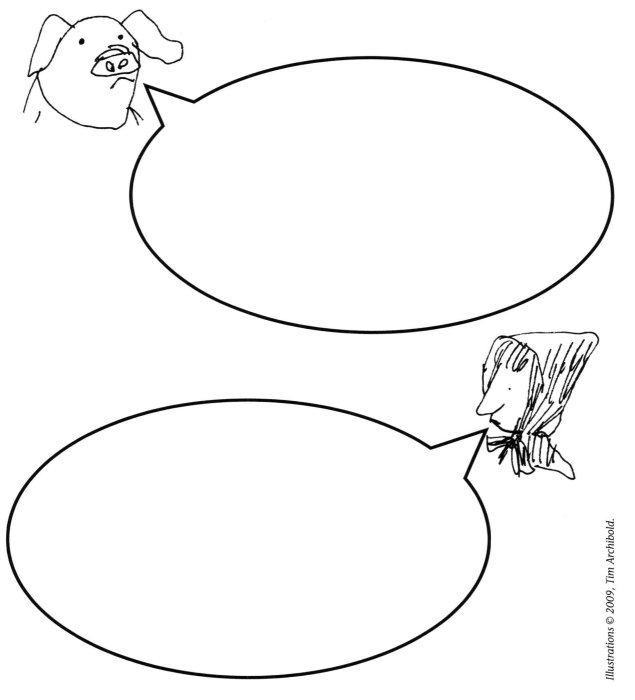

Illustrations © 2009, Tim Archibold.

Wicked ideas

● Most fairy stories have a character who plots something bad. What do you imagine these characters are thinking?

Illustrations © 2009, Tim Archibold.

Cinderella's feelings

● Fill in the speech and thought bubbles in these two scenes.

Illustrations © 2009, Tim Archibold.

Describe the setting

● Look at the pictures in the 'Media resources' file of the CD-ROM. Draw a picture of one of the places in the box below.

```


```

● Imagine you are in the setting. Complete the sentences below.

```
I can see
```

```
I can hear
```

```
I can smell
```

```
I feel
```

writing guides

Who lives here?

● Look at the pictures in 'Media resources' on the CD-ROM. Draw a picture of one of the places in the box below.

Write about who might live in this setting.

Write about what might happen in this setting.

Order the story

- Cut out and put the pictures in the correct order.

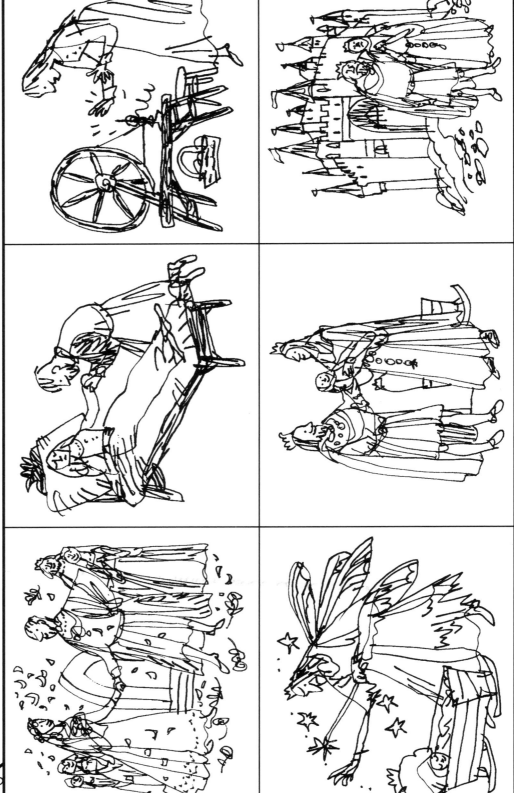

Illustrations © 2009, Tim Archibold.

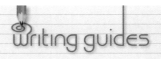

writing guides

The plot

● Complete a plot breakdown for a fairy story of your choice.

Title _____

Characters	Setting	Story opening
Problem	Resolution	Ending

Here we go again!

- Plan your own fairy story with three characters.

Title _____

Characters

1	2	3

- Complete the storyboard below to show three events that will happen in your story.

1	2	3

Section 3

Writing

Creative process

Having read a wide range of fairy stories, explored many of the key features of the fairytale genre and after completing the activities in the previous two sections, the children should now be ready to embark on writing their own fairy stories.

The three writing projects in this section provide opportunities for the children to plan and write complete fairy stories. The activities provide a framework for developing children's skills, knowledge and confidence as story writers.

The timescale for completing the three extended writing activities will need to be fairly flexible. In order to progress from initial ideas to finished stories, the children will require a number of extended writing sessions. Some children will enjoy returning to work previously started, while others find it difficult to pick up from where they left off and will need support in restarting and redrafting their work.

Map out the sessions

The three extended writing activities outlined in this section all follow a similar format. Each activity provides opportunities for:

- oral work . The children are given opportunities to discuss and rehearse ideas orally, in small groups or with a partner.

- shared writing. You will model how to use a number of simple planning frames to plan ideas for new fairy stories and then help the children turn the ideas in the shared story plans into written text using the 'My story' writing templates on the CD-ROM.

- independent work. The children repeat the work undertaken in the shared session, independently, planning and writing their own fairy stories. Children can either present their stories on-screen using the 'My story' writing templates on the CD-ROM or on paper as a piece of extended writing.

Providing support

Provide targeted support for all the children as they plan and write their own stories.

Encourage them to consider how they might refine and improve their plans and first drafts using prompts from the poster on photocopiable page 18 'Fairy tales' or by referring to the interactive version of the poster on the CD-ROM. Refer to the activities completed in previous sessions so that the children can draw on their knowledge and experience of a range of fairy stories read in class.

Writing tips

When writing a fairy story:
- write in the third person and past tense
- use formulaic openings and endings ('Once upon a time...')
- make sure the story has a clear beginning, development and ending
- set the story long ago
- include good and bad characters
- use phrases drawn from story language ('she disappeared in a puff of smoke')
- use time words to sequence events
- use description and repeated dialogue to make the story interesting for the reader.

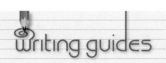

Project 1: Pick a card

Objective

To select from different presentational features to suit particular writing purposes on paper and on screen (Year 2 Strand 8). To use key features of narrative in their own writing (Year 1 Strand 9).

What's on the CD-ROM

Pick a card – characters
- Select fairytale characters.

Pick a card – settings
- Select a fairytale setting.

Story planner
- Complete the story planning frame.

My story
- Compose a story using a writing template.

What to do

This activity teaches the children how to plan and write a fairy story using the 'My Story' writing templates on the CD-ROM.

- Copy and cut out a set of character and setting cards from photocopiable pages 38 and 39 'Pick a card'. Hold up each of the cards in turn and ask the children to name the character or setting pictured on each card and to give a brief description. Invite children to help you sort the cards into three bags labelled 'Good characters', 'Bad characters' and 'Settings'.

- Tell the children that you would like them to help you plan and write a story with a good character, a bad character and a fairytale setting. Choose children to come out to the front and pick a card (one from each bag) to determine the characters and setting to be used in the shared story. Alternatively, use the 'Pick a card – characters' CD-ROM file. (Note: the blue cards indicate good characters and the red cards indicate the bad. The activity lets you to pick two characters at a time). They can also use the CD-ROM activity 'Pick a card – settings', this activity allows you to pick one setting at a time.

- Open the CD-ROM file 'Story planner' (by clicking on the 'Planning' button in the main menu). Complete the four screens of the planner together. Type in details of the chosen setting and the characters. Ask children to discuss ideas for the story opening, events and ending. Record the children's ideas in the planning frame. Finally, discuss and agree on a suitable title for the story.

- Open the CD-ROM file 'My story'. Click on one of the writing templates to open a new page. Explain that this is going to be the first page in your story. Demonstrate how to insert and resize an image from the 'Image bank'. Next, using ideas suggested by the children, type in a simple story opening which describes the story setting and introduces the characters.

- Open a new page (template) and continue writing the story. Involve the children as much as possible when selecting images, orally drafting and then writing appropriate text in the text boxes. (Note: where suitable images are not available in the 'Image bank' they can be uploaded.)

- Look at the other writing tools available on the tool bar. Where appropriate, show children how to add speech or thought bubbles. In pairs, let them draft text for the bubbles onto individual whiteboards.

- When the story is complete, read and evaluate it with the children in terms of content and presentation features.

- Let each child randomly select a good character, a bad character and a setting for their story using the 'Pick a card' activities (see above). Give each child a copy of photocopiable page 41 'Story planner'. Ask them to plan and write their own fairy story using the setting and characters they have picked.

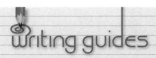

Project 2: Story starter

Objective

To use key features of narrative in their own writing (Year 1 Strand 9).

What's on the CD-ROM

Story starter
- Complete a story plan.

My story
- Compose a story using the writing template.

Story planner
- Plan, compose and write their own version of a fairy tale.

What to do

The purpose of this activity is to encourage children to plan and write their own fairy story using a familiar patterned story as a model for writing.

- Read a version of 'Jack and the Beanstalk' to the children. Briefly recap the characters, setting and sequence of events.

- Open the CD-ROM file 'Story starter'. Discuss possible answers to each question on to generate ideas for a new story. Type in some of the children's ideas to produce a simple story plan. You could also give each child a copy of photocopiable page 40 'Story starter' to complete if they wish to work on paper.

- Open the CD-ROM file 'My story' (instructions of how to use this file are in the notes for Project 1). In shared writing, demonstrate how to use the plan to compose and write a story. Involve the children as much as possible in the writing process.

- Give all the children a copy of photocopiable page 41 'Story planner'. Ask them to plan, compose and write their own version of 'Jack and the Beanstalk'. They can also do this on screen by navigating to the 'Story planner' via the 'Planning' button in the main menu.

Project 3: Fairy story map

Objective

To use planning to establish clear sections for writing (Year 2 Strand 10).

What's on the CD-ROM

Fairy story map
- Image bank: Discuss who might live in each setting and what might happen.
- Complete a story plan.

Media resources
- Audio clip: Discuss who might live in the wood and what might happen.

My story
- Compose a story using the writing templates.

What to do

This activity asks children to plan and write their own fairy story.

- Open the CD-ROM file 'Fairy story map'. Tell the children that they are going to complete the text boxes together. Ask the children to imagine they are walking along a path leading to each question.

- Encourage the children to name and describe the first setting. Using the written prompts ask the children to imagine who lives in the castle and what they might be doing.

- On each screen encourage the children to give imaginative responses to the prompt questions. Use the on-screen tools to record some of the children's ideas. Where appropriate, look at the photographs or images (in 'These images' from the 'Image bank') and use the audio clip in the 'Media resources' section of the CD-ROM, to reinforce the nature of the settings.

- Give the children copies of photocopiable pages 42 and 43 'Fairy story map'. Ask the children to plan a story that includes three different settings: a castle, a wood and a final setting of their own choice. They should then use their planning sheet to create their own fairy story, either as a piece of extended writing or by using the writing templates in the 'My story' section of the CD-ROM (see notes for Project 1).

Pick a card – characters

Bad

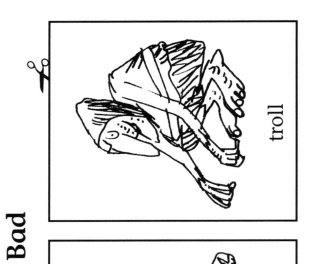

troll

wolf

giant

witch

Good

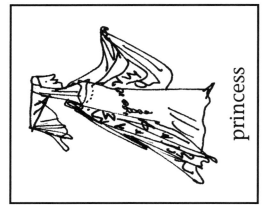

princess

little girl

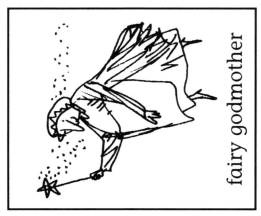

fairy godmother

little boy

Illustrations © 2009, Tim Archibold.

Writing guides

Pick a card – settings

Story starter

● Imagine you find a magic beanstalk at the bottom of your garden. Start at the bottom and climb to the top.

What happens?

Who do you meet?

How do you feel?

Where does the beanstalk lead to?

Illustrations © 2009, Tim Archibold.

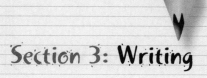
Story planner

● Plan and write your own fairy story.

Setting	

Characters	

Story opening	

Main events		

Ending	

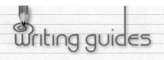

Fairy story map

Who lives in the castle?

What happens in the castle?

Why are they
hiding?

Who is hiding in the
wood?

Who is on the path?

Where does this
path lead?

Illustrations © 2009, Tim Archibold.

Section 4
Review

Evaluate progress

Ongoing formative assessment of children's learning in writing is essential. It allows teachers to evaluate the progress that children are making towards achieving specific learning targets and to plan the next steps in learning at an appropriate level. It is also important to make an overall review of children's progress at the end of a unit of work to review work against national standards and identify gaps in teaching and learning.

Self-review

In order to involve pupils fully in their learning it is important that they are included as much as possible in the assessment process. Photocopiable page 45 'Self review' is a self-assessment tool designed to be used by the children working independently, to review how successful they have been in using some of the characteristic style/language features of the fairy-tale genre in their own writing. You may wish to model the self-review process first, using one of the shared stories created by the whole class.

Peer review

Photocopiable page 46 'Peer review' encourages the use of writing partners to help children review and develop their written work. Organise the children to work with a partner of similar ability. Instruct them to read and then review their partner's fairy story by answering the questions on the photocopiable page. Provide opportunities for feedback. Ask each child to tell their partner what they liked about their story and give advice about how they think it could be improved. Remind children that their comments to each other should be constructive and supportive.

Teacher review

The grid on photocopiable page 47 'Teacher review' has been designed to enable you to record evidence of pupils' progress and attainment in writing at the end of a unit of work on fairy stories. It is linked to the National Curriculum's eight assessment focus objectives for writing. When reviewing children's work in relation to each assessment focus, it is important to use a range of evidence. This could include observation (What contributions did the child make in speaking and listening and drama activities in, for example, 'Cinderella's feelings'?) as well as assessment of children's written work.

Carrying out such a review will enable you to evaluate the progress individual children have made towards achieving specific learning goals. The review findings should be used to set group and individual learning targets and to ensure that the next steps in learning for all children are planned at an appropriate level. The review may also highlight gaps in teaching and learning. If this is the case, identify and teach/revisit the relevant lesson(s) in Section 2 of this guide to address these gaps.

Self review

My fairy story is called _____

Fairy-story language

I use this sentence to begin my story:

Describing words

I use these describing words to make my writing interesting for the reader:

Time words

I use these time words to link the main events in my story:

Dialogue

One of my characters says:

Sentence structure

I have written in sentences.   ☐ yes   ☐ no

I have used capital letters and full stops.   ☐ yes   ☐ no

Peer review

● Answer these questions to review your partner's fairy story.

Story title: _____

Written by: _____

Beginning	A fairytale setting and characters are introduced.	☐ yes ☐ no
Middle	One of the main characters has a problem. Something happens to resolve the problem.	☐ yes ☐ no
End	The story has a happy ending.	☐ yes ☐ no

● Does the story have all the elements of a fairytale plot?

☐ yes ☐ no

● Has the writer remembered to use describing words to make their story interesting for the reader?

☐ yes ☐ no

● What did you like best about the story?

_____

● Describe one way you could improve the story.

_____

Teacher review

	AF5 Vary sentences for clarity, purpose and effect	AF6 Write with technical accuracy of syntax and punctuation in phrases, clauses and sentences.	AF3 Organise and present whole texts effectively, sequencing and structuring information, ideas and events	AF4 Construct paragraphs and use cohesion within and between paragraphs	AF1 Write imaginative interesting and thoughtful texts	AF2 Produce texts that are appropriate to the task, reader and purpose	AF7 Select appropriate and effective vocabulary	AF8 Use correct spelling
LEVEL 1	Uses appropriate time connectives to begin sentences from alternatives supplied. Mainly simple grammatically accurate statements.	Some use of full stops and capital letters indicates awareness of basic punctuation. Clauses are mostly grammatically accurate.	Attempts to sequence ideas in chronological order. Some attempt to use formulaic story openings and endings from a word bank.	Some events and ideas linked using repeated nouns/ pronouns	Basic information about characters and events communicated through relevant words and phrases. Some simple descriptive vocabulary.	Some use of key features of narrative in own writing, with support.	Simple descriptive language is used, e.g. to describe characters.	Most simple high frequency words spelt correctly. Attempts to spell unknown words phonetically.
LEVEL 2	Generally consistent use of past tense. Time connectives used to vary sentence openings. Uses a mixture of simple and compound sentences with clauses joined by *and* and *then*.	Use of full stops and capital letters to demarcate sentences are generally accurate. Some exclamation and question marks used correctly.	Simple narrative with an opening, development and ending. Uses time related words and phrases to sequence or connect events. Formulaic openings and/or endings are used in story writing.	Uses simple planning frames to create clear sections for writing. Some ideas linked by simple pronouns.	Mostly relevant content and ideas. Uses patterns and language from familiar stories to add interest.	Some typical language and organisational features of fairy tales used in own writing. Attempts to use appropriate writing style.	Use of appropriate vocabulary with some words used effectively. Some attempt to use story language.	Most high frequency grammatical function words spelt correctly. Spelling reflects increasing awareness of whole word structure, visual patterns and letter strings.

writing guides

SCHOLASTIC

Also available in this series:

ISBN 978-1407-11253-4

ISBN 978-1407-11265-7

ISBN 978-1407-11267-1

ISBN 978-1407-11256-5

ISBN 978-1407-11270-1

ISBN 978-1407-11248-0

To find out more, call: **0845 603 9091**
or visit our website: **www.scholastic.co.uk**